CANAPÉS
MADE EASY

ABIGAIL BROWN AND MELISSA WEBB

STERLING PUBLISHING CO., INC.
NEW YORK

Published in the United States in 2003 by
Sterling Publishing Company, Inc.
387 Park Avenue South, New York, N.Y. 10016

Distributed in Canada by Sterling Publishing
c/o Canadian Manda Group, One Atlanntic Avenue, Suite 105
Toronto, Ontario, Canada M6K 3E7

Original edition published by New Holland Publishers (UK) Ltd.

Library of Congress Cataloging-in-Publication Data Available

ISBN 184330 4139

Senior Editor: Clare Sayer
Production: Hazel Kirkman
Design: Roger Hammond
Photographer: John Freeman
Editorial Direction: Rosemary Wilkinson

Based on a design idea by Michele Gomes.

1 3 5 7 9 10 8 6 4 2

Reproduction by Colourscan, Singapore
Printed and bound by Times Offset (M) Sdn Bhd, Malaysia

ABI

I dedicate this book to the four men in my life: Samuel, Alexander, Matthew, and Barnaby Brown. May they grow up with a love of good food and fine wine like their Auntie Abi!

MELISSA

I only have one man in my life, Tim, and thank him for being there through the tears and sweat and I hope he has enjoyed the giggles!

ABI and MELISSA

have worked together for eight years, starting in the grueling location-catering world.

Abi went on to be a food critic for Egon Ronay as well as traveling extensively, collecting invaluable culinary experience.

Melissa stayed in the location world then set up a catering company six years ago, which they both work in now. Having known each other since they were at school, they are a great team and are loved by all their clients.

CANAPÉS

MADE EASY

CONTENTS

INTRODUCTION

Canapés are defined in some old dictionaries as pieces of fried French bread spread with pâté or some such ingredient. Well, how they have changed! As you read this book you will realize that canapés are not as dull as this definition suggests. They are tempting mouthfuls of flavor and color, each a little meal in itself.

None of the recipes in this book are difficult to prepare—it is the attention to flavor, color, and presentation that make these canapés look and taste so delicious!

We have tried to use a wide range of different foods, giving you a selection of meat, fish, and vegetarian canapés to serve to your guests.

The reasons for giving a party are to get friends and family together and for the sheer enjoyment of it. A party should never be hard work or a hassle. Using these recipes you should find you are able to prepare and serve a wide range of delicious canapés to your guests and still enjoy the party. With various tips on presentation and styling your friends will be amazed at your culinary skills.

Canapés can set the tone for your party from the very beginning. Delicious mouthfuls, served with an aperitif before dinner, put us all in a good mood for the evening ahead. If, on the other hand, they are, as it were, the main event on occasions when a full meal does not follow the party, then eye-catching and fragrant nibbles, such as Stem ginger and king shrimp skewers, Quail's egg, basil and sun-dried tomato skewers or Garlic bruschetta with rare roast beef and cilantro cream cheese, will tempt the taste buds and more than compensate for lunch or dinner. They can help the conversation along and make your party all the more memorable.

We have both traveled extensively, tasting and cooking food all over the world, and our cooking has drawn on the valuable influences from a worldwide cuisine. We both have a passion for cooking and have worked together over many years. We have designed, created and made hundreds of different canapés for occasions both great and small. This book offers just a small selection of these and we hope you enjoy preparing, making, serving, and, of course, eating them! Perhaps when you have mastered some of the recipes in the pages that follow, you can use your imagination and flair to adapt and create your own canapés!

Bon appétit!

EQUIPMENT

A good craftsman can always work better with the right tools. It is not essential to have a huge selection of kitchen equipment to prepare canapés but a few key items will help get the job done quicker and make life much easier for you. Here are a few utensils we can't do without in our kitchen:

KITCHEN KNIVES It's not necessary to rush out and buy a block of expensive knives, one for every job, but two or three good sharp knives will make chopping much easier. Generally we use three different knives: a small vegetable knife with a smooth blade, a small serrated knife, and a large 8-inch chopping knife. It is important to keep your knives sharp and clean. Store them safely in a knife case or block. This keeps them out of harm's way and keeps the blades sharp. Of course, a sharpening steel is essential to keep the blades sharp. If you don't know how to use one or can't bear the noise, your local butcher may show you or even sharpen your knives for you!

CHOPPING BOARD In a proper catering kitchen we have to use plastic chopping boards for hygienic reasons but at home you can have plastic or wooden. We find the plastic boards easier to use because they are easier to keep clean and they do not retain the smell of garlic or onion. (There is nothing worse that cutting fruit on a board that tastes faintly of garlic!) If you do buy a plastic board choose one that is quite thick as the weight helps to hold it still when you are chopping (alternatively, you can put a tea towel under the board to hold it still). When you wash a plastic board make sure it is dried properly as it can smell if left damp. Of course wooden boards are still widely used—it is just a matter of preference.

POTS AND PANS Stainless steel heavy-bottomed pans are the best to use. They are easy to clean and very durable. You can slowly build up a collection of different sizes as you get more into your cooking. A non-stick frying pan and small saucepan are always very useful, especially if you are making scrambled eggs or frying pieces of salmon. If using non-stick pans make sure you do not use metal utensils but heatproof plastic or wooden ones instead.

BAKING SHEETS AND TRAYS It is useful to have two or three non-stick baking sheets and trays because they are essential for easy cooking. Do not use metal spatulas or utensils on non-stick trays.

SCALES AND MEASURING CUPS It's important to have some good kitchen scales, electronic or manual, and measuring cups so that your recipes are accurate. Measuring spoons are also useful when it comes to small quantities.

ELECTRIC APPLIANCES None of these pieces of equipment are essential but they do make cooking much easier:
- A hand-held electric whisk for whipping cream.
- An electric juicer for lemon or orange juice.
- A food processor is a fantastic piece of equipment for the kitchen, saving time when you are grating, mixing, chopping herbs, and many other things.
- And last but by no means least, a good mixer is great for mixing, whipping cream, liquidizing and many other jobs.

PALETTE KNIVES A very useful utensil for levelling the top of desserts (like the Créme brûlée spoons on page 70) or for gently lifting canapés off a baking tray.

PLASTIC SPATULAS The best thing to get all the mixture out of the mixing bowl without using your fingers. Now they are heat-proof and can be used in frying pans or woks.

SQUEEZE BOTTLES Usually found in a kitchen shop, the squeeze bottle is great for dropping small amounts of sauce on to canapés like the ketchup on the Mini sausages with potato purée (see page 54) for instance.

A few other utensils we find useful to have in the kitchen are: a good pair of tongs, salad spinner, metal mixing bowl, assorted cookie cutters, citrus zester, blowtorch (for caramelizing sugar), kitchen scissors, plenty of wooden and metal spoons, a good plastic piping bag with a variety of nozzles, baking parchment, foil, and plastic wrap.

INGREDIENTS

It is always a good idea to have a few basic ingredients stored in your kitchen so that if uninvited guests turn up at your door you can quickly whip up some tasty canapés.

We have listed some of the things that we like to keep to hand but that doesn't mean you should rush out and buy them all at once! You will slowly build up a well-stocked kitchen, depending on what your personal favorites are. It's always a good idea to have a good selection of fresh vegetables about so you can make a dip with crudités. Some varieties are perfect for canapés, especially miniature vegetables such as cherry tomatoes and baby corn. Fresh herbs are always a lovely thing to have on your kitchen window ledge, they look good, smell lovely and can make all the difference to your canapés. Every kitchen should have garlic, of course, good-quality olive oil, sea salt, and freshly ground black pepper. All these things make the bases for good cooking! Buy little and often so that your ingredients don't go out of date—the fresher and better quality your ingredients are the better the end result!

Kitchen Cupboard

Balsamic vinegar

Olive oil

Canned water chestnuts

Sweet soy sauce

Sweet chilli sauce

Pine nuts

Stem ginger

Cranberry sauce

Canned butter beans

Canned cannelloni beans

White wine vinegar

Sun-dried tomatoes in oil

Runny honey

Kitchen Shelf

Fresh garlic

Basil plant

Parsley plant

Fridge

Parmesan cheese

Cream cheese

Feta cheese

Unsalted butter

Lemons

Thai green curry paste

Mustard (grainy mustard and Dijon are probably the most useful)

Freezer

Cocktail sausages

Chicken livers

Sfilatino (thin, uncooked ciabatta—takes about 20 minutes to defrost)

Filo pastry

Dumpling pastries

Kaffir lime leaves (these keep well in the freezer and only need minutes to defrost before using)

Fresh ginger (keeps better in the freezer than in the fridge)

Frozen green peas (petit pois are sweeter and more flavorful)

PRESENTATION

Presentation is crucial with canapés. They should look good as well as taste delicious.

These days there are so many interior and kitchen shops that sell amazing plates, bowls, boards, and dishes that there is no excuse for bringing out dreary aluminum trays and lining plain plates with white doilies. If you have taken the trouble to make beautiful canapés you might as well make them look as good as possible on some attractive trays and stylish dishes.

White ceramic plates and dishes are classy and timelessly elegant, and just use the canapés as decoration. Or you could experiment with different ideas. Use colored napkins under your food to bring out a particular color in it.

If your canapés have an Oriental theme maybe use some banana leaves underneath them or bamboo matting. Don't just use plain white ramekins for dips and sauces, shop around and get some small, shallow, colorful dipping bowls. Chinese and Japanese food shops usually have some great bowls and plates that are ideal for serving party food. If you live in an area with many different cultures try looking in some of the different food shops, Thai, Indian or African, and see if they have some interesting fruits or flowers that you could use to decorate your serving dishes.

Use your imagination to put your individual mark on your party. You will see as you read though this book that we have served some of the canapés on different dishes, with bright napkins, white china spoons and beautiful dipping bowls, all of which add to the overall effect. This is how you need to present your food. Your guests will be impressed by your imagination and style, and will appreciate the effort you have taken.

It is best not to bring all the food out all at once, or to put dishes around the room on small tables with wobbly legs. Much better to hand your canapés around personally, or ask some helpers to do so. Make sure that the helpers know what is on each dish, and enjoy moving around the room hearing the gasps of delight at your culinary expertise. For an evening drinks party we would normally estimate that you need about six to eight "bites" per person, but it all depends on your opinion of your guests' appetites, financial considerations, and the nature of the party.

PASTRIES

TURKEY AND CRANBERRY FILO PARCELS

makes 20

INGREDIENTS

1 lb skinless, boneless turkey
  breast

salt and pepper

1 tbsp chopped flat-leaf parsley

2 tbsp cranberry jelly or sauce

1 tbsp heavy cream

butter for melting

1 packet good-quality filo pastry

EQUIPMENT

food processor

pastry brush

baking sheet

Pre-heat the oven to 350˚F.

Season the turkey with salt and pepper, cover with foil to keep in the moisture and place in a roasting tin. Roast in the oven for about 15 minutes or until cooked all the way through.

When the turkey is cooked lift out of the roasting tin, reserving the cooking juices. Allow the meat to cool a little, and then roughly chop. Place the chopped turkey, parsley, cranberry jelly, and cream in the food processor and blend. If the mixture seems too dry add some of the cooking juices. Do not over-blend: the mixture should be chunky rather than smooth, and slightly wet but not soggy.

Melt a little butter for the filo pastry. You may need to melt a little more as you go on.

Take a sheet of filo, brush with a little melted butter and layer another sheet of filo on top. Brush again with butter and cut into 2 in squares. Repeat until you have 20 squares.

Take a heaped teaspoon of the cooled turkey and cranberry mixture and place in the middle of the pastry square

Take the top and bottom of the left side of each pastry, and the top and bottom of the right side and gather them up together. Then join these together so that you end up with a square parcel.

Brush the finished parcels with melted butter, lay on a baking sheet and cook for 10 minutes until golden brown.

These can be made in advance and frozen uncooked. Allow to defrost for 1 hour before baking.

MUSHROOM AND TARRAGON FILO PARCELS

makes 20 **INGREDIENTS** 1 large garlic clove, crushed; 1 lb chopped mixed mushrooms; 6 tbsp butter plus extra for melting; juice of 1 lemon; dash of brandy; 2 tsp chopped fresh tarragon; 1 tbsp heavy cream; salt and pepper; 1 packet filo pastry; sesame seeds **METHOD** Pre-heat the oven to 350°F. Fry the garlic and mushrooms in the butter. Add the lemon juice and brandy and place in a blender with the cream and tarragon. Process until the mixture is chunky. Allow to cool before making the filo parcels. Brush with butter and sprinkle with sesame seeds before baking.

FILO PARCELS WITH SMOKED CHICKEN AND APRICOTS

makes 20: **INGREDIENTS** 2 tbsp butter, melted; 12 oz smoked chicken; 4 oz dried apricots; 2 tbsp cream cheese; 1 scallion, chopped; salt and pepper; 1 packet filo pastry **METHOD** Pre-heat the oven to 350°F. Put half the melted butter, the smoked chicken, apricots, cream cheese, scallion, and seasoning into the blender and blend. The mixture should be chunky and slightly wet, but not soggy. Allow the mixture to cool before making the filo parcels. Brush with melted butter and cook for 10 minutes or until golden brown.

FILO PARCELS WITH SALMON AND CHERVIL

makes 20 **INGREDIENTS** 1 lb salmon; 2 tbsp chopped fresh chervil or dill; 1 tbsp grated fresh horseradish; 2 tbsp cream cheese; salt and pepper; 1 packet filo pastry; butter for melting **METHOD** Pre-heat the oven to 350°F. Cover the salmon with foil and poach on top of the hob for 20 minutes or until cooked and flaky. Allow to cool. Place the chervil or dill, horse-radish, cream cheese, and salmon in the blender and process. The mixture should be chunky rather than smooth. Season with salt and pepper and make into parcels as above.

FILO PARCELS WITH SPINACH, FETA AND PINE NUTS

makes 20 **INGREDIENTS** butter for melting; 1 tbsp pine nuts; 12 oz spinach; 4 oz feta cheese, mashed; salt and pepper; 1 packet filo pastry; oil for frying **METHOD** Pre-heat the oven to 350°F. Melt a little butter in a non-stick pan and brown the pine nuts briefly. Take care, as they brown quickly. Remove and set aside. Wilt the spinach in a little butter, using the same pan. When the spinach is cooked squeeze out any excess juices and chop roughly. Mix the feta into the spinach, add the pine nuts and season lightly. Make into round filo parcels and deep-fry until golden brown.

PORK AND CHESTNUT DUMPLINGS

makes 20

INGREDIENTS

14 oz pork fillet, trimmed

4 oz can water chestnuts, drained

1 tbsp sweet soy sauce

2 cloves garlic, crushed

2 kaffir lime leaves, finely sliced

2 tsp sugar

salt and pepper

2 chillies, deseeded and finely
    chopped

flour for dusting

20 round sheets dumpling pastry

oil for frying

soy sauce or sweet chilli sauce,
    to serve

EQUIPMENT

mixer

pastry brush

absorbent paper towel

METHOD

Put all the ingredients except the dumpling pastry sheets and the sweet chilli sauce into the mixer and process. The mixture should be chunky rather than smooth. Check the seasoning, it should be sweet.

Sprinkle a work surface with flour and lay out as many pastries as you can. Using a pastry brush, brush a little water around the edge of each circle.

Put a teaspoon of the filling in the middle of each pastry. Fold over the edges and seal to make a semi-circle. Make three pinches at equal distances around each semi-circle to make the dumplings more attractive.

Heat the oil in a large, heavy-bottomed pan. It should not be too hot, as you need the pork inside to cook as well as the pastry. Deep-fry for about 5 minutes and then drain on paper towel. Serve with sweet chilli sauce.

Variation: **CHICKEN AND CILANTRO DUMPLINGS** makes 20 **INGREDIENTS** 1 lb chicken breast; 2 tbsp chopped cilantro; 1 tbsp sweet soy sauce; 1 tsp sesame oil; 2 cloves garlic, crushed; 2 shallots, finely chopped; 2 tsp sugar; salt and pepper; flour for dusting; 20 round sheets dumpling pastry; soy sauce, to serve; 2½ cups chicken stock **METHOD** Put all the ingredients except the pastry sheets, soy sauce, and stock in a food processor and blend until chunky; check the seasoning. Make the dumplings as above. Heat the stock in a pan and poach the dumplings for 5 minutes or until they are cooked through.

CARAMELIZED RED PEPPER AND ROSEMARY TARTLETS

makes 20

INGREDIENTS

3 red peppers

8 tbsp unsalted butter, plus extra
 for caramelizing the peppers

2 sprigs fresh rosemary

1 tbsp superfine sugar

4 sheets filo pastry

8 tbsp cream cheese

3 oz Gorgonzola

EQUIPMENT

pastry brush

round cookie cutter

small shallow muffin tray

METHOD

Pre-heat the oven to 400°F.

Slice the peppers into thin strips, removing all the membrane, and then gently cook with a knob of butter, one sprig of rosemary, and the superfine sugar. The idea is to slowly caramelize the peppers, without allowing them to color. They will ooze some liquid, which is good and adds to the flavour. This will take about half an hour to 40 minutes.

Meanwhile, melt the butter and brush the filo sheets. Layer two sheets together and cut out rounds with a cookie cutter. Gently place the pastry rounds in the muffin tins and cook for 5 to 8 minutes until golden brown.

Mix the cream cheese and Gorgonzola together until smooth.

To assemble, put a teaspoon of the cheese mixture into the pastry shell. Take a couple of strips of caramelized pepper and curl them onto the top, then garnish with rosemary.

These may be served warm or cold but do not let them sit around for too long or the pastry will go soggy.

The pastries, red peppers and cheese mixture can be made in advance and stored separately in airtight plastic containers.

Alternative filling: **CHICKEN AND LEEK** Poach 1 lb skinless, boneless chicken breast for 10 to 15 minutes. Reserve the poaching liquid. Gently fry 1 lb shredded leeks in a little butter until soft. Make a roux sauce using 2 tbsp unsalted butter, 1 tbsp flour and the reserved poaching liquid. Chop the chicken and add to the sauce with the leeks. Season and spooon into the filo shells (see above) and garnish each with a sprig of parsley.

FILO BISCUITS WITH WHITE BEAN AND EGGPLANT PUREE

makes 20

INGREDIENTS

2 eggplants

4 garlic cloves, unpeeled

2 tbsp butter, plus extra for

   melting

1 onion, finely chopped

3 oz canned butter beans

3 oz canned cannellini beans

juice of 2 lemons

½ packet filo pastry

oil for frying

EQUIPMENT

baking sheet

mixer

pastry brush

2 frying pans

absorbent paper towel

METHOD

Pre-heat the oven to 350˚F.

To make the purée, place the eggplants and whole, unpeeled garlic cloves on a baking sheet and roast gently in the preheated oven for 30 minutes until soft. Remove from the oven.

Gently fry the onion in butter with the butter beans and cannellini beans.

Scoop out the eggplant pulp and squeeze out the garlic cloves from the skins. Place the eggplant pulp and roasted garlic cloves in the mixer with the lemon juice and the onion and bean mixture. Process until nearly smooth.

To make the filo biscuits, layer four sheets of filo, cut into strips measuring 3 in by 1 in, on top of each other with melted butter in between.

Heat the oil in a heavy-bottomed frying pan and deep-fry the filo biscuits until golden brown. Drain on paper towel.

Serve the eggplant and white bean purée in a bowl in the center of a serving dish, with the filo biscuits around it. Provide a spoon for scooping up the purée.

Both the purée and the biscuits can be made up to 3 days in advance, but the biscuits must be kept in well-sealed airtight containers. If they have gone slightly soft simply reheat them quickly for a couple of minutes in the oven to make them crisp again.

POACHED QUAIL'S EGGS WITH HOLLANDAISE IN PASTRY CUPS

makes 20

INGREDIENTS

dash of white wine vinegar

butter for melting

4 sheets filo pastry

20 fresh quail's eggs

2 egg yolks

2 tbsp white wine vinegar

salt and pepper

8 oz unsalted butter

1 sprig fresh tarragon

EQUIPMENT

saucepan

pastry brush

small shallow muffin tray

slotted spoon

METHOD

Pre-heat the oven to 350˚F.

Put a saucepan of water on to heat and add a dash of white wine vinegar. Keep on a low simmer.

Brush the filo sheets with a little melted butter. Layer two sheets together and cut out rounds.

Gently place the pastry in the muffin tins and bake in the preheated oven for 5 to 8 minutes until golden brown.

Carefully crack the quail's eggs into the water in the saucepan and poach for 2 minutes. The yolk should still be runny.

Remove with a slotted spoon and trim off and discard any excess cooked egg white. Set the poached quail's eggs aside.

To make the hollandaise sauce, put the egg yolks, white wine vinegar, salt, and pepper in the food processor and blend for about 2 minutes.

Melt the butter and add to the egg mixture in a thin stream as slowly as you can (the slower the better). The sauce will thicken as more of the butter is added. Add a little chopped tarragon to the hollandaise, reserving some for the garnish.

When you are ready to serve, place a quail's egg in the pastry cup and top with a little hollandaise. The sauce should fill the cup, but take care not to overfill. Pop the filled pastry cups in the oven for 5 minutes and serve garnished with tarragon. The pastry cups can be made in advance and kept in an airtight container. The eggs can be poached a day in advance and kept in the fridge, well covered.

Note: It is very difficult to make a small amount of hollandaise so you will have some left over—perfect with poached salmon.

SKEWERS

QUAILS' EGG, BASIL AND SUN-BLUSHED TOMATO SKEWERS

makes 20

INGREDIENTS

20 quails' eggs, hard-boiled

20 sun-blushed tomatoes

20 large basil leaves

celery salt

EQUIPMENT

20 skewers

METHOD

Hard-boil the quails' eggs for 2 minutes.

Drain and run under cold water. Peel the eggs straight away, as it is easier to remove the shells.

Cut the eggs in half but keep the pieces together.

Thread half a quail's egg on to a skewer followed by a sun-blushed tomato, then the basil leaf and, finally, the other egg half.

Sprinkle a little celery salt over the skewers for flavor.

Note: You can buy ready-boiled quails' eggs in jars in some supermarkets. These are fine for this recipe, and make the preparation much quicker.

Variation: **MOZZARELLA AND CHERRY TOMATO SKEWERS** makes 20

INGREDIENTS 20 red cherry tomatoes, 20 yellow cherry tomatoes, 20 mini mozzarella balls (boccocini), 20 skewers **METHOD** Thread a red tomato onto each skewer, then a mozzarella ball then a yellow tomato. These are extremely simple to assemble, but the effect is very pretty. Note: To add extra flavor, you could marinate the boccocini in some olive oil with fresh basil leaves and a little salt and pepper before using.

CILANTRO CHICKEN
ON LEMON GRASS SKEWERS

makes 20

INGREDIENTS

4 skinless, boneless chicken
   breasts

1 small bunch cilantro

2 red chillies, diced

4 kaffir lime leaves, thinly sliced

12 lemon grass stalks

2 tbsp fish sauce

2 tbsp dried breadcrumbs

oil for deep-frying

sweet chilli sauce, to serve

EQUIPMENT

food processor

heavy-bottomed frying pan

absorbent paper towel

METHOD

Place the chicken, cilantro, chillies, kaffir lime leaves, 2 of the lemon grass stalks, and fish sauce in the food processor. Process until smooth.

Put the chicken mixture in a bowl and mix in the breadcrumbs very thoroughly. They will bind the mixture together.

Prepare the lemon grass skewers by peeling off the outer layer of the remaining 10 lemon grass stalks. Trim both ends at an angle so you almost get a sharp point and then cut each stalk in half.

Heat the oil for deep-frying in the frying pan.

Take a generous teaspoon of the chicken mixture and mold into a ball using your hand. Carefully put it into the oil. Fry gently for 5 minutes.

Drain on absorbent paper towel and then skewer each ball onto a lemon grass stalk.

Serve with a sweet chilli dipping sauce.

The chicken mixture can be made up to two days in advance. The chicken balls can be fried 3 hours before serving and then heated in the oven just before serving.

STEM GINGER AND SHRIMP SKEWERS

makes 20 **INGREDIENTS** 1 small jar stem ginger; 20 fresh, uncooked large shrimp; butter for frying **EQUIPMENT** 20 wooden skewers, soaked in water for 15 minutes **METHOD** Put all the stem ginger and juice from the jar in a food processor and blend until smooth. Put 4 tablespoons of this mixture into a bowl and add the shrimp. You can return the rest to the jar and keep it in the fridge—it is great for adding to stir-fries. Make sure the shrimp are coated in the ginger. Leave to marinate for 2 hours, preferably overnight. Heat enough butter to fry the shrimp in a non-stick frying pan. Add the shrimp, about 5 at a time, and cook until they turn slightly golden, about 5 minutes. Thread the shrimp onto the skewers and serve immediately.

CILANTRO SHRIMP ON LEMON GRASS SKEWERS

makes 20 **INGREDIENTS** 20 lemon grass stalks; 5 tbsp finely chopped fresh cilantro; 1 tbsp superfine sugar; 2 tbsp fish sauce; butter for frying; 20 fresh, uncooked large shrimp **METHOD** Prepare the lemon grass skewers by peeling off the outer layer. Trim both ends at an angle so you almost get a sharp point. Mix the cilantro, sugar, and fish sauce together in a bowl. Toss the shrimp in the mixture and leave to marinate for 2 hours, preferably overnight. Heat enough butter to fry the shrimp in a non-stick frying pan. Gently fry the shrimp, about 5 at a time, until they turn pink, about 5 minutes. Thread each shrimp onto a lemon grass skewer, taking care not to push the shrimp too far up, or it will split. Serve immediately.

MOROCCAN LAMB FILLET ON ROSEMARY SKEWERS

makes 20 **INGREDIENTS** 1 tbsp ground cumin; 1 tbsp ground turmeric; 1 tbsp brown sugar; 1 tbsp hazelnut oil; 2 garlic cloves, crushed; 1 tbsp chopped fresh cilantro; 2 star anise, ground; salt and pepper; 2 lb lamb fillet, cut into strips; 1 small bunch fresh mint, chopped; ½ cup Greek yogurt; vegetable oil for shallow-frying; 20 large rosemary stalks **METHOD** Mix together the first seven ingredients in a large bowl and season. Add the lamb strips and marinate for at least 2 hours, preferably overnight. Mix together the chopped mint and yogurt. Thread the lamb onto the rosemary stalks and fry over a high heat in a little vegetable oil until dark brown. Serve with the yogurt and mint dip in a bowl.

THAI FISH FONDUE

You can use any kind of fish for this fondue, mussels, salmon, shrimp, monkfish, cod, snapper—whatever you like. Just cut all the fish into thin strips so they cook quickly in the stock. Shrimp and mussels can be cooked as they are.

serves 20

INGREDIENTS

For the stock:

$2\frac{1}{2}$ to $3\frac{1}{2}$ cups fresh fish stock
   (available from most supermarkets)

2 tbsp grated fresh ginger

1 red chilli, roughly chopped

4 garlic cloves

2 lemon grass stalks, cut into
   chunks

4 kaffir lime leaves

2 tsp green Thai curry paste

salt

1 small bunch fresh cilantro

selection of prepared fish

EQUIPMENT

fondue set

METHOD

Put the fish stock into a small saucepan and heat.

Add the grated fresh ginger, chilli, garlic, lemon grass, lime leaves, and Thai curry paste.

Simmer gently so all the flavors infuse the stock. This should take about 15 minutes.

Pour the stock into the fondue pan and add the fresh cilantro.

Invite your guests to skewer their chosen pieces of fish and cook them in the stock—this should take about 3 to 4 minutes.

CHICKEN FONDUE WITH PESTO DIP

serves 20 **INGREDIENTS** 5 skinless, boneless chicken breasts; salt and pepper; 2 bunches fresh basil; 2 garlic cloves; 5½ oz Parmesan cheese; 2 tbsp pine nuts; ¾ cup olive oil; vegetable oil to fill the fondue bowl **METHOD** Cut the chicken into thin strips and season with salt and pepper. Put the basil, garlic, Parmesan, pine nuts, and olive oil in a food processor and blend until smooth. Transfer the pesto to a bowl. Fill your fondue bowl with vegetable oil and heat. Take great care when using a fondue set with oil and make sure it is on a stable surface. Thread the chicken strips onto metal skewers for your guests to cook in the hot oil. Once cooked, the chicken can be dipped into the pesto before eating but take care as the chicken will be hot.

TORTELLINI WITH SPICY TOMATO DIP

serves 20 **INGREDIENTS** 1 small white onion, finely chopped; 1 tbsp olive oil; 1 small can chopped tomatoes; 1 garlic clove, crushed; 1 small red chilli, chopped; 1 tbsp tomato purée; salt and pepper; 2½ cups fresh vegetable stock; 1¼ lb fresh tortellini (with any filling) **METHOD** To make the spicy tomato dip, gently fry the onion in the olive oil until soft. Add the garlic and chilli and fry gently. Add the tomato purée and canned tomatoes. Cook on a low heat for about 5 minutes, then season to taste. This dip can be served hot or cold. Pour the stock into the fondue pan and heat. Thread the tortellini onto the skewers and lower into the simmering stock—they should take about 3 to 4 minutes if the stock is simmering gently.

CLASSIC CHEESE AND BREAD FONDUE

serves 20 **INGREDIENTS** 1 garlic clove, peeled; 1 lb Gruyére, diced; 2 tbsp potato flour; 1 glass white wine; pinch of grated nutmeg; salt and pepper; 2 tbsp kirsch; 1 stick French bread, cut into 1 in cubes **METHOD** Rub the inside of your fondue dish with a cut garlic clove. Cover the diced cheese with the potato flour and set aside. Pour the white wine into a small pan and heat. When the wine is hot add the floured cheese. As the cheese begins to melt, whisk it gently—melt the cheese slowly. Add the nutmeg and season to taste. Add the kirsch at the last minute, then pour the cheese mixture into your fondue bowl and keep it over a low heat and don't allow it to boil. Skewer the bread chunks with skewers and dip them in the hot fondue mixture.

PAN-FRIED SALMON SKEWERS WITH HOLLANDAISE

serves 20

INGREDIENTS

1 lb salmon fillet

3 tbsp chopped fresh basil

3 tbsp chopped fresh dill

3 tbsp chopped fresh chervil or
 parsley

juice of 2 lemons

salt and pepper

olive oil for frying

FOR THE HOLLANDAISE:

2 egg yolks

2 tbsp white wine vinegar

salt and pepper

8 oz unsalted butter

EQUIPMENT

food processor

20 wooden skewers, soaked in
cold water for 15 minutes

non-stick frying pan

METHOD

Cut the salmon fillet lengthways into small rectangular pieces about 3 in long and 1 in wide.

Mix all the herbs and lemon juice together in a bowl and season to taste.

Toss the salmon pieces in the herb and lemon juice mixture and leave for about 1 hour to absorb the flavors. If you are preparing in advance, do leave to marinate overnight as the flavor will be superb.

While the salmon is marinating, make the hollandaise. Put the egg yolks, white wine vinegar, and salt and pepper to taste in the food processor and blend for about 2 minutes.

Melt the butter and add to the egg mixture as slowly as you can (the slower the better). The sauce will thicken as more of the butter is added.

You can flavor your hollandaise with a little lemon juice or some more fresh herbs or just serve it plain. Once all the butter has been added put the sauce into a dipping bowl or ramekin.

Heat some olive oil in a non-stick frying pan.

Gently fry the salmon pieces on all sides until they are golden brown. If the salmon is very fresh it is nice to leave it a bit pink in the middle as it gives a better flavor.

Remove the salmon from the pan and allow to cool.

Carefully thread the salmon onto the wooden skewers and serve with the hollandaise sauce.

DIPS

SWEET POTATO CHIPS WITH SOUR CREAM AND CHILLI SAUCE DIP

INGREDIENTS

5 sweet potatoes, peeled

2½ cups vegetable oil for
   deep-frying

4 tbsp sour cream

1 small bottle (1¼ pt) sweet chilli
   sauce

EQUIPMENT

heavy-bottomed frying pan

METHOD

Cut the sweet potatoes into ½ in thick sticks, as straight as possible. You can use the excess potato for mash.

Heat the oil in the frying pan. You can test the temperature of the oil by dropping in a little piece of sweet potato. If the oil is hot enough the potato should float to the top and start to cook immediately.

While the chips are frying, place the sour cream into a small dipping bowl or ramekin so that it fills one side of the dish. Pour the sweet chilli sauce in to fill the other side.

Drain the cooked chips thoroughly on absorbent paper towel and stack them up on a plate. Serve with the sour cream and sweet chilli sauce dip.

Note: To prepare these in advance, simply pre-fry and then reheat in a hot oven for 10 minutes before serving.

CRAB CAKES WITH LIME AND TOMATO SALSA

serves 20

INGREDIENTS

FOR THE CRAB CAKES:

7 oz fresh white crabmeat

5½ oz puréed potato

2 kaffir lime leaves, thinly sliced

1 in piece fresh ginger, grated

juice of 2 limes

2 red chillies, finely chopped

1 tbsp fish sauce

FOR THE SALSA:

2 plum tomatoes. deseeded and
    finely diced

juice of 2 limes

2 tbsp soy sauce

2 tbsp roughly chopped fresh
    cilantro

½ red onion, finely diced

FRYING INGREDIENTS:

oil, as required

2 eggs

flour for dusting

dried breadcrumbs

EQUIPMENT

large, heavy-bottomed frying pan

METHOD

Combine all the ingredients for the crab cakes. Shape into balls and then pat flat into cakes. Put in the fridge to set.

Meanwhile, mix together all the salsa ingredients in a bowl and set aside.

Whisk the eggs and put into a shallow bowl and place the flour and the breadcrumbs into separate bowls too. Heat the oil for frying.

Coat the crab cakes first in flour, then beaten egg and finally breadcrumbs.

Fry until the breadcrumbs are golden brown. Serve the crab cakes hot or warm with the salsa on the side for guests to dip.

Note: these fish cakes can be frozen without the egg, flour and breadcrumb coating as long as the crab is fresh. Do not freeze if the crabmeat was previously frozen.

TEMPURA SHRIMP WITH LIME AND SESAME DIP

serves 20

INGREDIENTS

20 peeled large uncooked shrimp

4 oz flour for coating

FOR THE TEMPURA BATTER:

4 oz all-purpose flour

1 egg

1 cup iced water

FOR THE DIP:

juice and zest of 4 limes

1 tbsp sesame oil

1 tsp toasted sesame seeds

2 tsp light soy sauce

oil for frying

EQUIPMENT

heavy-bottomed frying pan

absorbent paper towel

METHOD

Make the tempura batter by mixing the flour, egg, and water together. The consistency should be lumpy.

Toss the shrimp in the coating flour and then roll in the batter mix.

Mix together the lime, sesame seeds, sesame oil, and light soy sauce.

Heat enough oil for deep-frying in a heavy-bottomed frying pan and fry the prawns until golden brown, about 4 to 5 minutes.

Drain on absorbent paper towel and serve immediately with the dip.

Note: most supermarkets and Chinese shops sell ready-prepared tempura batter, which is just as good as home-made if you prefer.

Variation **TEMPURA VEGETABLES WITH WASABI DIP** serves 20 **INGREDIENTS** tempura batter ingredients (see above); a of selection of vegetables, such as broccoli, strips of red pepper and baby corn; 4 oz flour for coating; 3 tbsp mayonnaise; wasabi paste (this is very hot so only use about a pea-sized amount; oil for frying **METHOD** Make the tempura batter as above. Cut your vegetables into small pieces and toss in the coating flour and then the batter. Mix the mayonnaise with wasabi to taste, adding a little more if it is not hot enough. Deep-fry the vegetables until golden brown. Drain on absorbent paper towel and serve immediately.

DIPS FOR COCKTAIL SAUSAGES

Serve your cooked cocktail sausages with any of the dips below. Try asking your butcher for flavored sausages, such as chicken and leek, lamb and mint, or wild boar.

MUSTARD MAYONNAISE DIP (OPPOSITE)

makes 1 small bowl **INGREDIENTS** 4 tbsp good-quality mayonnaise; 2 tbsp whole-grain mustard; **METHOD** Combine the mayonnaise and mustard and serve in a dipping bowl or ramekin.

SWEET AND SOUR DIP

makes 3 tbsp **INGREDIENTS** 1 tbsp olive oil; 1 tbsp clear runny honey; 1 tbsp tomato purée; 1 tsp brown sugar; 2 tbsp Worcestershire sauce; 2 tbsp soy sauce; salt and pepper **METHOD** Put all the ingredients into a small, heavy-bottomed pan and heat gently until the sugar is dissolved. Cook for about 10 minutes, until reduced to a syrup, season and serve hot or chilled.

CHILLI TOMATO DIP

makes 3 tbsp **INGREDIENTS** 1 small onion, chopped; 1 tbsp olive oil; 6 tbsp canned chopped tomatoes; 1 garlic clove, crushed; 1 small red chilli, finely chopped; 1 tbsp tomato purée; salt and pepper; **METHOD** Gently fry the onion in the oil until soft. Add the garlic and chilli and fry gently. Add the tomato purée and tomatoes. Cook over a low heat, season and serve hot or cold.

HONEY AND MUSTARD DIP

makes 3 tbsp **INGREDIENTS** 2 tbsp clear runny honey; 2 tbsp whole-grain mustard: **METHOD** Mix the honey and mustard together and serve in a small ramekin or dipping bowl.

SPOONS

OYSTERS

If buying oysters from your fishmonger, ask him to loosen the oysters from their shells for you to make life easier. Make sure they are very fresh and are kept in the fridge or on ice. Don't keep open oysters out of the fridge for more that 1 hour and if you are left with any opened oysters not used on the day throw them away.

OYSTERS WITH LEMON JUICE

serves 20 **INGREDIENTS** 20 fresh rock oysters, loosened from their shells; 2 lemons **EQUIPMENT** 20 china spoons **METHOD** Cut the lemons into wedges, making sure you have removed all the pith and pips. Place an oyster on each spoon with a wedge of lemon so that your guests can squeeze fresh lemon juice over their oyster. Serve immediately.

OYSTERS WITH CHAMPAGNE

serves 20 **INGREDIENTS** 20 fresh oysters, loosened from their shells; ½ cup champagne **METHOD** Place an oyster on each spoon. Drizzle a teaspoonful of champagne over each oyster just before serving. Serve immediately.

OYSTERS WITH TABASCO

serves 20 **INGREDIENTS** 20 fresh oysters, loosened from their shells; few drops of tabasco **METHOD** Place an oyster on each spoon. Carefully drop two or three drops of tabasco onto each oyster. Serve immediately.

OYSTERS WITH SHALLOT VINAIGRETTE

serves 20 **INGREDIENTS** 20 fresh oysters, loosened from their shells; 2 shallots; ½ cup red wine vinegar **METHOD** Finely dice the shallots and add to the red wine vinegar. Leave the vinegar to stand for about an hour to let the flavors develop. The shallot vinegar can be made the day before. Put a fresh oyster on each spoon and top with a teaspoon of the shallot vinaigrette. Serve immediately.

TEMPURA OYSTERS

serves 20 **INGREDIENTS** 4 oz all-purpose flour; 1 egg; 1 cup iced water; 20 fresh oysters, loosened from their shells; 4 oz) flour for coating; 2 limes, each cut into 6 wedges; oil for frying **METHOD** Make the tempura batter mixture by mixing the flour, egg, and water together. The consistency should be lumpy. Toss the oysters in the coating flour and then roll them in the batter mixture. Fry the oysters until golden brown, about 3 to 4 minutes, drain on kitchen paper and serve immediately with lime wedges for squeezing.

Note: most large supermarkets and Chinese food shops sell ready-made tempura batter, which is just as good as home-made.

CAVIAR WITH SOUR CREAM AND CHIVES ON SILVER SPOONS

Any type of caviar can be used for this canapé, depending how rich you are feeling! Lumpfish roe may be substituted.

serves 20

EQUIPMENT

20 silver teaspoons

INGREDIENTS

1½ oz Avruga caviar

3 tbsp sour cream

1 small bunch fresh chives, chopped

METHOD

Make sure the silver spoons are clean and free from tarnish.

Fill each spoon with caviar.

Top with a small amount of sour cream.

Sprinkle a few chopped chives on to the sour cream and serve.

MINI SAUSAGES WITH POTATO PURÉE

serves 20

INGREDIENTS

2 large white potatoes

salt and pepper

knob of butter

2 tbsp heavy cream

10 cocktail sausages (any flavor)

2 tbsp tomato ketchup

2 tbsp French (Dijon) mustard

EQUIPMENT

20 china spoons

METHOD

Boil and mash the potatoes and season to taste. Add the knob of butter and stir in the cream.

While the potatoes are boiling grill the cocktail sausages until golden brown and cooked through. Cut the sausages diagonally in half.

Spoon a little mashed potato onto each china spoon and place half a sausage into each spoon of mash.

Squeeze a little drop of mustard and ketchup onto each spoon. (A squeeze bottle or the end of a teaspoon is the best piece of equipment to use for this job.) Serve warm.

MUSTARD MASH

Make this recipe exactly as above, adding 2 tbsp of wholegrain mustard to the mashed potatoes.

SPRING ONION MASH

Make this recipe as above, adding 5 finely chopped scallions to the mash. Reserve a little chopped scallion to garnish.

SWEET POTATO MASH

Make this recipe as above, using 2 large sweet potatoes instead of white potatoes.

BREADS

BRUSCHETTA TOPPED WITH PEA AND MINT

makes 20

INGREDIENTS

8 oz frozen green peas, defrosted

1 tbsp boursin (garlic and herb

   cream cheese)

3 tbsp cream cheese

2 scallions, chopped

juice of 1 lemon

1 small bunch fresh mint

2 thin French baguette

olive oil for brushing

about 20 sprigs fresh mint

EQUIPMENT

food processor

METHOD

Preheat the oven to 400°F.

Place the peas, boursin, cream cheese, scallion, lemon juice, and mint leaves into a food processor or blender and pulse until blended but not smooth. The mixture needs to have texture! Place in the refrigerator for 30 minutes to chill.

Cut the sfilatino into rounds about 1 in thick and brush with a little oil.

Place on a baking tray and bake in the oven for about 5 minutes or until golden brown. Alternatively, you can grill them if you prefer.

Spoon a little of the pea paste onto each bread round and garnish with a tiny sprig of mint.

BRUSCHETTA WITH ASSORTED MUSHROOMS AND TRUFFLE OIL

makes 20 **INGREDIENTS** 20 bruschetta rounds (see page 57); 7 oz mixed mushrooms (oyster, shiitake); knob of butter; 3 tbsp truffle oil; salt and pepper **METHOD** Slice the mushrooms and fry in the butter. Season with salt and pepper and add 2 tbsp of the truffle oil. Put the mushrooms in a mixer and pulse—the mixture should have some texture and not be too smooth. Spoon the mushroom mixture on to the bruschetta slices and drizzle a little truffle oil onto each one to serve.

BRUSCHETTA WITH PARMESAN, CELERIAC AND BASIL

makes 20 **INGREDIENTS** 20 bruschetta rounds (see page 57); 10 oz celeriac; 3 tbsp heavy cream; salt and pepper; 4 tbsp grated Parmesan; 20 basil leaves **METHOD** Peel the celeriac and cook in boiling salted water for about 15 minutes. Mash with the cream and salt and pepper. Add the Parmesan and mix well. Spoon the mixture on to the bruschetta slices and garnish each with a basil leaf.

BRUSCHETTA WITH THREE-BEAN PATE

makes 20 **INGREDIENTS** 20 bruschetta rounds (see page 57); 10 oz canned butter beans, drained; 10 oz canned broad beans, drained; 4 tbsp cream cheese; 3 scallions, finely chopped; 3½ oz green beans, cooked and finely chopped; salt and pepper **METHOD** Put the butter beans, broad beans, cream cheese, and spring onions into a mixer and process until chunky (not smooth). Mix in the finely chopped green beans and season with salt and pepper. Spoon the mixture onto the bruschetta and serve.

BRUSCHETTA WITH TOMATO AND BASIL

makes 20 **INGREDIENTS** 20 bruschetta rounds (see page 57); 4 fresh plum tomatoes; 2 tsp tomato purée; 2 tsp superfine sugar; 1 clove garlic, crushed; salt and pepper; 1 small bunch fresh basil **METHOD** Cut the flesh from the tomato and discard the core and seeds. Finely dice the flesh and put into a mixing bowl. Add the tomato purée, sugar, and garlic and season with salt and pepper. Chop a few basil leaves into the mixture. Spoon onto the bruschetta slices and garnish each with a fresh basil leaf.

GARLIC BRUSCHETTA WITH RARE ROAST BEEF AND CILANTRO CREAM CHEESE

makes 20

INGREDIENTS

2 sticks thin French baguette

3 tbsp olive oil, plus extra for frying

2 garlic cloves crushed

5½ oz fillet of beef

1 small bunch fresh cilantro

3 tbsp cream cheese

salt and pepper

EQUIPMENT

large, heavy-bottomed frying pan

METHOD

Pre-heat the oven to 350˚F.

Cut each bread stick into 10 slices.

Mix the olive oil and crushed garlic together.

Sprinkle the garlic and oil mixture over the bread slices.

Bake in the preheated oven for 4 to 5 minutes until golden brown. Set aside to cool.

Heat a little oil in the frying pan. When the pan is hot add the beef fillet and pan-fry for about 2 minutes each side.

The beef should be rare in the middle. If you do not like your meat as rare as this cook it for a little longer, but the flavor won't be as good.

Cut the meat into tiny squares.

Pick a handful of cilantro leaves from their stalks and chop finely.

Mix the cilantro with the cream cheese and season with salt and pepper to taste.

Spread the garlic bruschetta slices with the cilantro cream cheese mixture and top each with a piece of rare beef.

Garnish with a cilantro leaf.

BREAD CUPS FILLED WITH SCRAMBLED EGGS AND BACON

makes 20

INGREDIENTS

7 thin slices granary bread

5 tbsp butter, melted

4 slices streaky bacon

3 eggs

dash of heavy cream

salt and pepper

EQUIPMENT

2 in round cookie cutter

mini muffin tin

small saucepan

METHOD

Pre-heat the oven to 350˚F.

Cut the crusts off the bread and roll the bread flat with a rolling pin.

Using the cookie cutter, cut 20 circles out of the bread and brush with a little of the melted butter. Push the bread circles into the individual molds of the muffin tin. Cook until golden brown around the edges. This should take about 4 minutes. Remove from the oven and set aside to cool.

Grill the streaky bacon until golden brown then cut into tiny thin strips. Set aside.

Make the scrambled egg at the very last minute just before you are about to serve. Put the remaining melted butter in a small saucepan and warm gently. Whisk the eggs and cream in a bowl and season to taste with salt and pepper. Pour the egg mixture into the pan and cook. Do not overcook, as the scrambled eggs are much nicer if they have a soft texture.

Fill the bread cups with scrambled egg and top with the bacon strips.

Serve immediately.

Alternative toppings:

SMOKED SALMON Top the scrambled egg cups with a ribbon of very thinly sliced smoked salmon and garnish with a small sprig of fresh dill.

SMOKED EEL Take a small packet of smoked eel (14 oz) and cut the eel into small triangular shapes. Top each scrambled egg cup with a triangle of eel and garnish with a small sprig of thyme.

BRIOCHE ROUNDS WITH SUNBLUSH TOMATOES AND PECORINO

makes 20

INGREDIENTS

5½ oz sunblush tomatoes

7 slices brioche (available from
   most supermarkets), 1 in thick

2 oz pecorino cheese, thinly shaved

EQUIPMENT

food processor

2 in round cookie cutter

baking sheet

METHOD

Pre-heat the oven to 350˚F.

Blend the sunblush tomatoes, with the oil they come in, in the food processor. Do not over-process—the tomato mixture should be chunky, not smooth.

Cut the brioche slices into 20 circles with the cookie cutter.

Place the brioche circles on a baking sheet and top with the sunblush tomato mixture. Bake in the preheated oven until the brioche is a golden brown color. This should take about 3 minutes.

Remove the brioche slices from the oven and garnish each circle with a shaving of pecorino.

Serve warm.

DESSERT CANAPÉS

CHOCOLATE BROWNIES

INGREDIENTS

9 tbsp unsalted butter

4½ oz plain chocolate

4 eggs

10½ oz sugar

4½ oz all-purpose flour

1 oz cocoa powder

1 tsp vanilla extract

2½ oz roughly chopped nuts, such
  as hazelnuts, almonds, walnuts

confectioners' sugar, to decorate

5 tbsp heavy cream, whipped

EQUIPMENT

greased baking tin (8 x 12 in) lined
  with baking parchment

medium saucepan or double boiler

electric whisk

METHOD

Pre-heat the oven to 350˚F.

In a medium saucepan or double-boiler melt the butter and chocolate together slowly. Stir gently until it is smooth.

Allow the chocolate mixture to cool for about 10 minutes

Beat the eggs and sugar in a mixing bowl until light and fluffy, using a hand-held electric whisk.

Gradually add the cooled chocolate mixture to the eggs and sugar, whisking all the time.

Fold the flour, cocoa powder, vanilla, and nuts into the egg and chocolate mixture.

Pour into your prepared baking tin and bake in the preheated oven for 30 minutes.

Allow to cool in the tin, then cut into small squares.

These brownies can be made in advance and kept in an airtight container for a couple of days, but they are better eaten on the day they are made.

Dust with confectioners' sugar just before serving and serve with a bowl of whipped cream.

RASPBERRY DIP WITH MERINGUE STICKS

makes 20

INGREDIENTS

10 oz fresh raspberries

3 tbsp confectioners' sugar

4 tbsp water

FOR THE MERINGUE:

4 egg whites

8 oz superfine sugar

EQUIPMENT

piping bag with a small round nozzle

baking sheet lined with baking parchment

small non-stick saucepan

METHOD

Pre-heat the oven to 200°F.

To make the meringue, put the egg yolks in a large metal mixing bowl and whisk, using a hand-held electric whisk, until the whites form soft peaks. Add the superfine sugar to the egg whites, a teaspoon at a time, whisking constantly.

Put the meringue mixture into the piping bag and pipe lines about 5 in long onto the baking sheet. Alternatively, pipe wiggly lines. Make sure there is a little bit of space between them, as they will expand as they cook.

Bake in the preheated oven for about 40 minutes until off-white in color then take out of the oven. Allow the meringue sticks to cool on the baking parchment then gently peel off.

Gently heat the raspberries with the water and confectioners' sugar in a small non-stick saucepan until softened.

Remove from the heat and liquidize in a blender. Push the purée through a sieve to remove all the seeds and then chill in the refrigerator.

Serve the meringue sticks with the chilled raspberry dip.

FRUIT SKEWERS WITH CHOCOLATE DIP Any fruit can be used for these fruit skewers but it is best to choose fruit that will stay on the skewers, such as strawberries or slices of kiwi fruit or star fruit. Be as exotic as you like in your choice! **CHOCOLATE DIP:** Place 7 oz good-quality plain chocolate with a knob of butter in a bowl placed over a pan of simmering water. Stir gently until it is smooth and melted. Alternatively, place in a microwave on a medium temperature for 1 minute; check and repeat until the chocolate is all melted. Serve immediately with the fruit skewers.

MINI CRÈME BRÛLÉE SPOONS

makes 20

INGREDIENTS

1 fl oz milk

8 fl oz heavy cream

1 vanilla pod or 3 drops vanilla
  extract

3 egg yolks

1½ oz superfine sugar for
  sprinkling

EQUIPMENT

ovenproof shallow dish

roasting tin

20 china spoons

saucepan

mixing bowl

blowtorch (optional)

METHOD

Pre-heat the oven to 300°F.

In a pan gently warm the milk and cream with the vanilla pod and seeds.

In a mixing bowl whisk the egg yolks and superfine sugar and gently add the cream mixture, discarding the vanilla pod.

Pour the mixture into an ovenproof shallow dish.

Stand the dish in a roasting tin filled with about 1 in of water.

Bake in the oven for about 45 minutes to 1 hour until the mixture is firm and no longer wobbles.

Remove from the oven and cool.

Once cool, spoon the brûlée onto the china spoons. Level the mixture with a palette knife.

Sprinkle the superfine sugar onto the spoons. If you have a blowtorch use it carefully to caramelize the sugar until it is golden brown. If you don't have a blowtorch heat your grill as high as it will go and caramelize the sugar under the grill until golden. Take care not to burn the sugar.

Allow to cool before serving or you will burn your guest's mouths!

The brûlée can be made up to 3 days in advance, the spoons assembled on the day but the caramelized sugar topping can be done only 1 hour before serving.

STRAWBERRY, BANANA, AND CRANBERRY JUICE

makes 20

INGREDIENTS

14 oz strawberries, hulled

5 bananas, peeled

4¼ cups cranberry juice

blueberries, to decorate

EQUIPMENT

blender

cocktail sticks

20 shot glasses

METHOD

You may need to prepare this recipe in two batches, as it may not fit in your blender all at once.

Put half of all the ingredients in the blender and mix until smooth and uniform in color.

Blend the other half and pour the smoothies into a jug and chill.

Pour into shot glasses and decorate the smoothies with a blueberry cocktail stick: thread two or three fresh blueberries onto a cocktail stick and serve in the smoothies as a stirrer. Add ice cubes if wished and serve immediately.

The blueberry cocktail sticks can be made in advance and frozen. Serve them straight from the freezer or defrost for about 10 minutes before serving.

MELON AND GINGER WHIP Liquidize the deseeded flesh of 2 ripe cantaloupe melons with 2½ cups fresh orange juice. Grate a 2 in piece of fresh root ginger and squeeze in your hand to extract the juice. Add to the melon and orange, a little at a time, tasting as you go (it is very strong). Chill and serve in 20 small shot glasses.

MANGO AND PASSION FRUIT SMOOTHIES Liquidize the flesh of 4 ripe mangos with 2½ cups fresh orange juice. Pour into a jug. Remove the seeds from 10 passion fruit and stir into the mango and orange. Serve chilled in shot glasses.

MENU PLANNING

The more organized you are before your party the more you and your guests will be able to enjoy it. There is nothing worse than going to a party when the hostess is rushing in and out of the kitchen all night and can't relax. With a little advance planning you can make sure that your party runs smoothly and that you get to enjoy it too.

All the canapés in this book are very simple and some can be prepared in advance to make life easier for you. It is very important not to overstretch yourself. Choose canapés that you think you will be able to make well. Make sure you have a good selection but don't overdo it by giving your guests too much choice. It's better to do eight canapés really well than 20 that are not quite right.

Take into account who is coming to your party. It will make your guests feel special if you have considered their dietary needs; perhaps you have vegetarian friends, or someone with a wheat intolerance or nut allergy. If you have a budget you may need to limit the number of guests you invite so you can buy enough food and drink for everyone to enjoy.

You may like to theme your party by choosing canapés from different countries, such as Thai, Indian or Italian. Take into account the age of your guests. Elderly people do not always appreciate too many spicy canapés, and if children are coming you may like to do something fun for them to have separately.

Think about how you will serve your canapés, what kind of plates you might use, the color of your napkins, glasses etc. If you plan ahead and think about these things you will have less to worry about on the day.

CATERING FOR LARGE NUMBERS

First of all, don't panic. Catering for large numbers doesn't have to be difficult, all it takes is just take a little extra planning.

Once you know how many people are coming to your party you may decide to enlist some help. Perhaps a friend who enjoys cooking may like to help you on the day.

Plan your menu and then decide what can comfortably be done in advance. Perhaps some items can be made up weeks before and frozen or prepared the day before the party and kept in the fridge.

If you are catering for large numbers don't make life difficult for yourself by choosing too many canapés to prepare. Stick to just a few, so you don't feel overwhelmed.

If your budget is tight, stick to the cheaper canapés, like cocktail sausages with various dips, or bruschetta with different toppings. You can also have some ready-made nibbles like roasted nuts, olives and potato chips for your guests to graze on.

You may like to hire a couple of waitresses, or if you have children perhaps they could be persuaded to lend a hand in passing the canapés around to your guests. Remember your party is as much for you as it is for your guests, so you need to be able to enjoy it and actually spend time with your visitors. Perhaps you could even hire a chef to put the canapés together, if your budget will stretch to it.

As long as there is plenty of delicious food and wine your guests will be happy and the party will be a huge success.

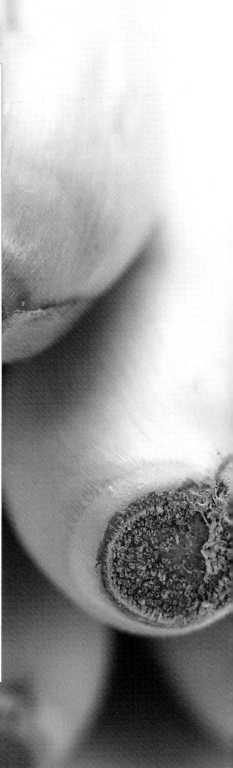
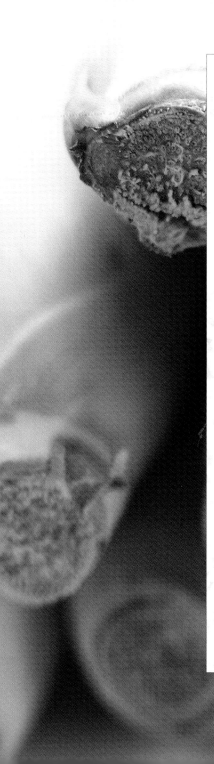

BUYING INGREDIENTS

When you shop for your ingredients, remember that the better the quality, the better the flavor. Nowadays there is so much choice in the supermarkets and market stalls that you can get almost all kinds of food all year round. Organic food is very popular at the moment as it has great flavor and color.

Try to buy your food as close to the day you need it as possible. The fresher it is, the better. Make sure when buying fruit and vegetables they are not bruised or discolored. If you are buying in the market, don't be afraid to choose your own ingredients.

There are so many different kinds of supermarkets now, Chinese, Indian and so on, that it can be fun to shop in different places and look at ingredients you haven't seen or cooked with before. Instead of using the nearest huge supermarket, perhaps try your local butcher, fishmonger and markets. You may not always get the cheapest ingredients but the quality and service is often better; your local butcher may cut different pieces of meat for you, or your fishmonger may prepare your fish for you, saving you time and hassle.

Make sure your food is stored properly, in the fridge or freezer if necessary or in a cool dark place. Your ingredients will last longer if they are correctly stored.

SUPPLIERS

Local markets are often the best place to buy good, fresh fruit and vegetables. Look out for organic produce, and exotic ingredients, as well as good fresh produce.

Farmers' markets, where producers and suppliers sell local produce direct to the public, are springing up all over the country. For details of a farmers' market near you, visit the USDA Farmers' Market website:

www.ams.usda.gov/farmersmarkets

INDEX

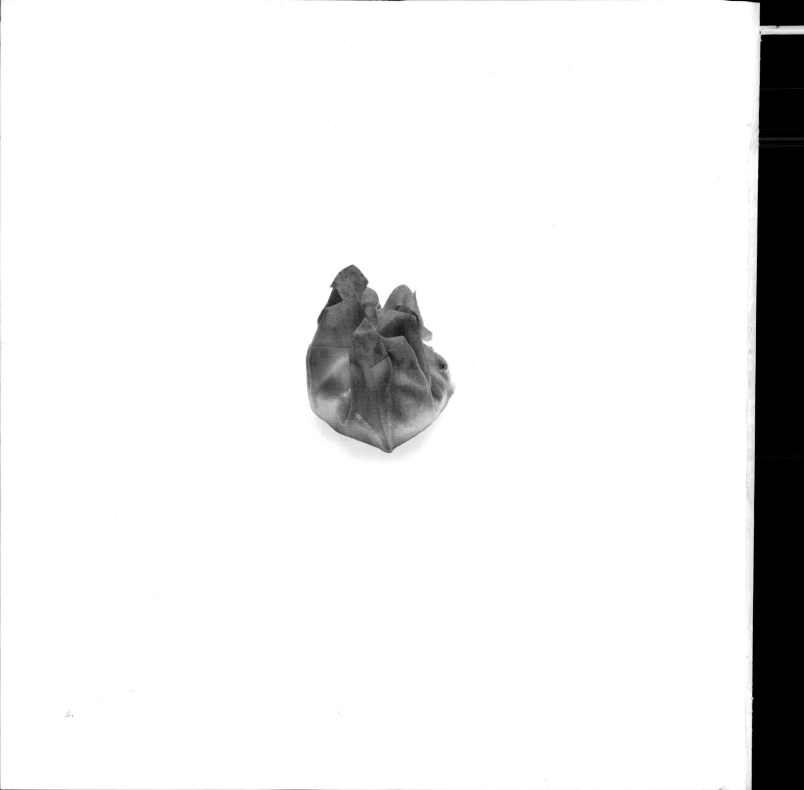